AF411861

The Dreamer Within

Prologue: The New Age of Dreams

We are awakening to a new age of dreams.

It is a time when the old dreams have failed us. The dreams that once seemed important—the dreams of progress, of power, of controlling nature to make it do our bidding—have turned into waking nightmares, which grow ever more ominous. And yet at the same time that the old dreams are failing—and perhaps just because they are—a vast new horizon of reality has come into ascendancy. Slowly, people everywhere are realizing that, unless we are to destroy ourselves, both personally and collectively, the goddess Reason—"our greatest and most tragic illusion," as Jung called her—who has for so long dominated our civilization, must be joined on her throne by her polar opposite, Intuition. And with this comes the realization that the real work to be done is the transformation of consciousness. This is the time of that transformation, and dreams are one of the main bridges to the New Age which that transformation will bring.

All of which helps explain the sudden renaissance of interest in the dream. In sleep laboratories around the world, dreamers are the subject of serious scientific research; in colleges, professors conduct classes on the psychology of dreaming; the literary marketplace and the media reflect the interest. Long considered helpful to patients undergoing psychotherapy but of little interest to so-called "normal" people, dream interpretation has come out of the consulting room and into the living room. Every person who sets out to work with his dreams is an adventurer in consciousness, a discoverer not only of his own inner truth but of a larger picture that is only just beginning to emerge. There has never been a more exciting time to explore the way of the dream.

Through the games and exercises that follow, you will be able to make contact with a very important being: the dreamer within. The dreamer within is that part of ourselves we do not know, but who knows us better than we know ourselves. It can lead you to the teacher within; the healer within; the creative, effective, spontaneous, and loving person within—the whole person you want to be. We present our material in the form of games and exercises, because we believe that the approach to the inner life must be one of humor as well as seriousness. Not that working with dreams is a frivolous pursuit; the unconscious will not yield up its secrets to those who take its dictates lightly or are unwilling to face up to the truths it will certainly expose. But neither is it a grim business. Being playful with our dreams, experimenting with them, inviting them warmly into our lives, we can be open to the joy of discovering our own self.

Act I: The Many Maps of Dreams

Although the maps of the dream world have not been fully charted—indeed, no one map could ever do it justice—there have been many preliminary surveys from which we can learn much. A look at some of these major theories about dreaming, from the healing temples of the ancient gods to the sleep laboratories of today's scientists, will set the scene for our practical work.

The Ancient World. Throughout the ancient world, dreams were thought to have an origin apart from the dreamer. They were conceived of either as reports from the soul, which might leave the body during sleep and wander in other realms, or as omens from the gods, good or bad. Many magical systems rose up to appease the gods who brought bad dreams and to curry advice and favor from those who brought good ones. To the dream-incubation temples of Serapis, the Egyptian god of dreams, and later to those of Aesculapius, the Greek god of healing, came thousands of pilgrims, seeking advice and healing. After rigorous periods of fasting, prayer, and sacred ritual they might sleep in the temple of the god and receive their longed-for dream. (Modern methods of dream incubation are discussed on page 6.) Plato, a mystic about dreams, saw them as a release for passionate inner forces; Aristotle debunked the idea of their divine origin, and another Greek, Artemidorous of Ephesus, produced in the second century the *Oneirocritica,* the encyclopedic progenitor of the thousands of "dream books" that have appeared down through the ages.

Dreams and Religion. The idea that God spoke to man more readily in dreams than in waking visions was a commonplace in the ancient world. Both the Old and New Testaments of the Bible are replete with dream messages and dream interpretations: the dream of Joseph and the sheaves; the Pharaoh's dream, which Joseph interpreted; Jacob's dream of the ladder between heaven and earth, and Joseph's dream that Mary would give birth to the Christ are only the most prominent examples. The Talmud, that storehouse of Hebrew practical wisdom, shows the importance the Jews gave to dreaming, and the high regard in which they held the dream interpreter: "An uninterpreted dream," wrote Rabbi Hisda, "is like an unopened letter." Not only was the religion of Islam based on the great initiatory dream of Mohammed, but the Prophet continued to rely on his own dreams and those of his disciples—whom he called together every morning to discuss their dreams—to formulate his ongoing teachings. In Moslem countries, dream interpreters had almost the status of holy men. During the late Middle Ages, dreams fell into disrepute; Christians sometimes feared they could be a door to the Devil and his works. By the late nineteenth century, dreams were being examined from a physiological perspective, and the ancient notion that

the gods spoke to men in dreams was dismissed as childish nonsense. Against this background of skepticism emerged the ground-breaking work of the first great modern explorer of the dream, Sigmund Freud.

The Analytic Maps: Freud and Jung. With the publication of *The Interpretation of Dreams* in 1900, Sigmund Freud, the Viennese psychiatrist who became the founder of psychoanalysis, brought the dream squarely into the scientific arena, where it would have to be dealt with from that time on. To very briefly sum up his theory, Freud saw the dream as a disguised wish-fulfillment of infantile sexual needs, wishes which, in waking life, would surely be repressed by the stern censor of the mind. Thus, the manifest or apparent content of a dream was only a facade for the real dream behind it—the latent dream whose contents would be so shocking to the dreamer that they would rouse him from his sleep (hence Freud's famed dictum that "dreams are the guardians of sleep"). By a complex process called the dream work, involving condensation (condensing several ideas into one image), displacement (switching of proper emphasis), secondary revision (creating order out of the chaos of the dream), and symbolism (largely sexual), the latent dream content manages to stay disguised. To interpret such a dream, a skilled interpreter—the analyst—was necessary to unravel the dream backward from its manifest content and, through the patient's free-associating with whatever came to mind, pierce the various veils to the unconscious materials.

It was such considerations, and particularly Freud's narrow view of the unconscious (he saw it as a kind of psychic garbage heap that had within it no seeds of the higher mental life) that troubled his one-time disciple-turned-dissenter, the Swiss psychiatrist Carl Jung. "Sigmund Freud," he wrote, "confirmed for most people the existing contempt for the psyche. Before him it had been merely overlooked and neg-lected; now it has become a dump for moral refuse. . . . The discovery that the unconscious is no mere depository of the past, but is also full of germs of future psychic situations and ideas, led me to my own new approach to psychology."

Unable to accept Freud's notions of the dream as wish-fulfillment, its predominantly sexual nature, and the theory of the disguise mechanism, Jung saw the dream instead as a compensatory mechanism, whose function was to restore one's psychological balance. His concept of the unconscious was much grander than Freud's: Beyond the personal unconscious, he wrote, lies a vast repository, the "collective unconscious," a part of the evolutionary tendency of the human mind, which links man with his primitive ancestors. Indeed, studying extensively primitive peoples and immersing himself in the study of their myths, dreams, and rituals, Jung found startling similarities in the unconscious contents and the symbolic processes of both modern man and primitives. In both he recognized the presence of archetypes—"mental forces whose presence cannot be explained by anything in the individual's own life and which seem to be aboriginal, innate and inherited shapes of the human mind."

It is crucial, said Jung, that the dreamer pay attention to the archetypes he meets in his dream life. Of special importance is the *shadow*, a figure of the same sex as the dreamer, which contains all the repressed characteristics one has not developed in his conscious life; the *anima*, the personification of all the female psychological tendencies, both positive and negative, in the male psyche, and its counterpart for the female psyche, the *animus*. The most significant, and most mysterious, of the Jungian archetypes is the *Self*, which, as M. – L. von Franz describes it in *Man and His Symbols*, is at once the "regulating center that brings about a constant expansion and maturing of the personality" and the fulfillment of that process, the "Cosmic Man" who "lives within the heart of every individual, and yet at the same time fills the entire cosmos." The Self emerges only when the ego can surrender and merge into it (Jung saw the Self as encompassing the total psyche, of which the ego is only a small part); thus, the individual completes the psychic integration of the personality, that striving toward wholeness which Jung calls "individuation."

Unlike Freud, Jung rejected any attempt to impose arbitrary interpretations on dreams. He accepted their manifest content, preferred to see them in series rather than alone, and dismissed free association as wandering too far afield from the dream content. He developed instead a system of "elaborations," in which the dreamer relates all that he knows about a symbol, as if he were explaining it, indeed, to a visitor from Mars.

Some Modern Maps: Edgar Cayce and Fritz Perls. Edgar Cayce, the American psychic who astounded the world during the 20s, 30s, and 40s with his extraordinary medical readings of thousands of individuals, also did extensive work on dreams. His teachings, which are still being studied today by dream researchers and adventurers at the Association for Research and Enlightenment (ARE) in Virginia Beach, Virginia, abound in both spiritual and psychological insights. For Cayce, whose work is discussed in detail in Elsie Sechrist's *Dreams—Your Magic Mirror*, the most important dreams come from the "superconscious . . . that portion of the mind [that] has retained the memory of God's presence. It is man's remaining tie and his communications link with his original spiritual consciousness." (I am reminded of Rudolph Steiner's beautiful saying that we do not sleep because we are tired, but we are tired because the soul wishes to return to its true home.) Cayce felt dreams from lower levels of the mind could also be helpful, since they can give us information on such matters as healing, diet, exercise, and on potential mental and emotional storms that will

The Separation

materialize unless we take preventive action.

The meaning of a dream, said Cayce, lies not in some theory but in the dream itself. Most people can learn to analyze their own dreams if they will give them proper attention, but there is no point in dream interpretation unless one sincerely wants to change his behavior, work on his spiritual development, and be of service to others. In that light, it is interesting to note that Cayce (and also Steiner) found the dream an accurate moral barometer of how well—or how poorly—one had done in that respect on the previous day.

More than thirty years after Cayce's death, the ARE is still in the vanguard of creative dream research. Those interested in partaking in an exciting dream community experience should look into *Sundance Community Dream Journal*, an experimental publication "designed to serve a circle of cooperative dreamers personally interested in educational dream research guided by spiritual ideals."

Fritz Perls, the Viennese-trained psychoanalyst who, in the 1950s and '60s became the veritable guru of the Human Potential movement, is known as the father of Gestalt therapy. Eschewing any theory of the unconscious, Gestalt therapy works with the personality as it is "here-and-now," seeking to complete the gestalt or wholeness in a person by reintegrating those parts of one that have been alienated. The dream is an existential message to oneself. The highly valuable technique of "gestalting" a dream will be discussed in detail on page 7.

Dreams in the Laboratory. The year 1953 marked a new kind of breakthrough in the study of dreams. Hooking subjects up to EEG machines which recorded both ocular patterns and brain-wave movements, sleep researchers at the University of Chicago discovered that dreamers exhibit patterns of jerky, rapid eye movements (REM) accompanied by a specific kind of brain-wave activity. Observing the brain-wave patterns, they learned that the REM periods—very short at the beginning of the night and increasingly longer toward morning—always occur in cyclical fashion, taking the sleeper from light into deep sleep and back up again on the average of four to seven times per night. Subjects awakened after REM periods invariably reported dreams. In hundreds of repeated experiments, other scientists have confirmed that everyone dreams every night. We know now that the average person spends about twenty percent of his or her sleep-time (about four and one-half years of his life) dreaming; and that the proportion of REM dreams is very high in infants, slightly less high in childhood, and lower in old age.

Studies in REM deprivation have shown that dreaming sleep is a physiological necessity; its omission over a long period of time can have negative psychological effects as well. Scientists have also monitored the products of non-REM sleep, concluding that, while mental activity occurs throughout the night, the "dreams" of non-REM periods are more likely to be colorless and unemotional compared to the intense activity of the REM states.

As a result of these studies, some cherished notions about dreams went down the drain. No longer could tangled bed sheets or indigestion be blamed for causing a dream, although they might indeed effect its contents. No longer could dreams be called the guardians of sleep; more often they were its disturbers. Since dream study came of age in the laboratory, scientists in many countries have been busy examining not only the biological aspects of dreams but also such paranormal experiences as dream telepathy, precognitive dreams, and ESP. For our purposes, however, the most important point is that there is no one who does not dream; and anyone who sincerely wishes to recall dreams can learn to do so, as we will show in the pages ahead.

What We Dream About. What do people dream about? Not patients in an-

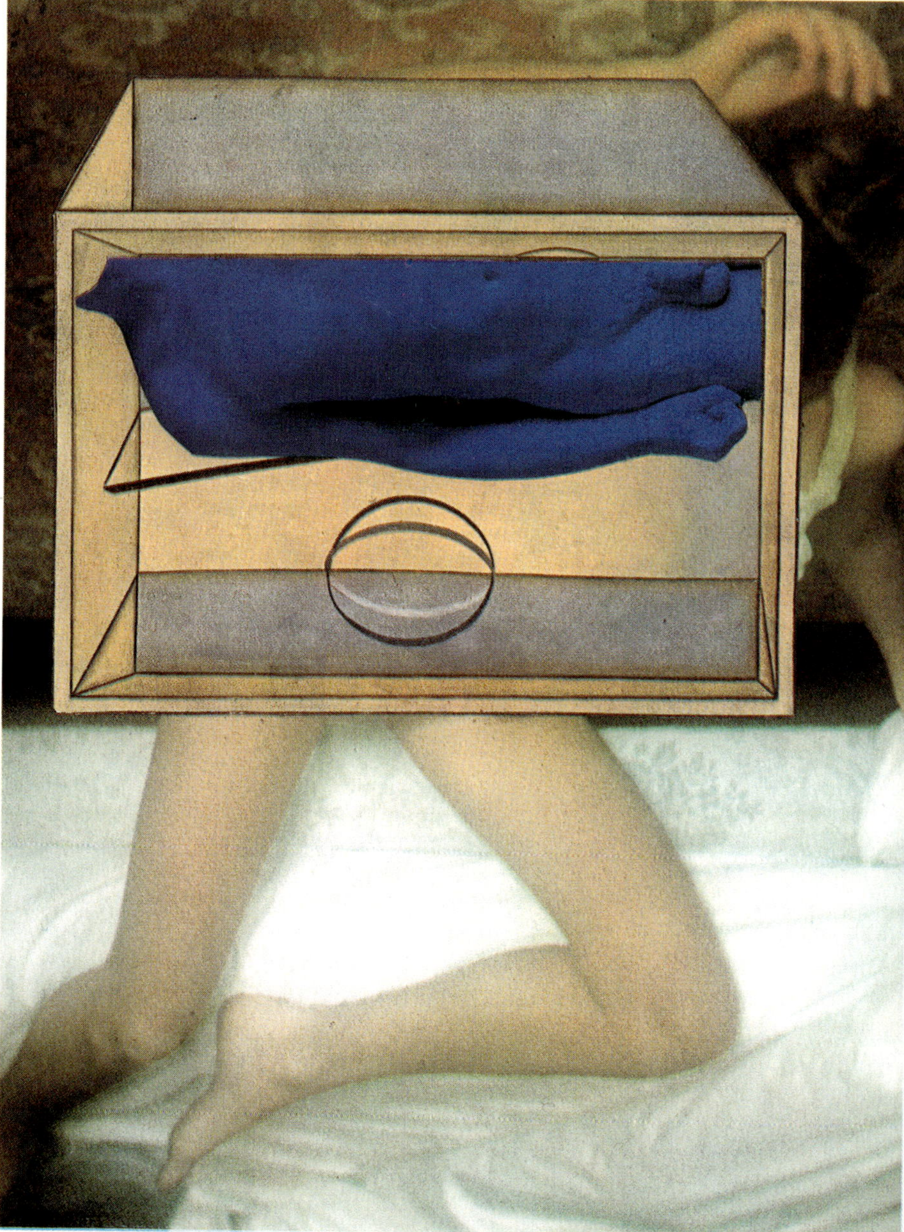

The First Invasion

lytic treatment, not subjects in sleep laboratories, but normal, everyday people like you and me? Psychologist Calvin S. Hall and a team of his associates at the Institute of Dream Research in Santa Cruz, California, set out to discover just that. Over a period of years, they analyzed and collected the dreams of some ten thousand people. In 1953, the same year as the biological breakthrough, Hall published *The Meaning of Dreams*, which showed that what we dream about is the one subject we're all the most interested in—ourselves. We dream about our private lives and innermost conflicts—conflicts relating to right and wrong, freedom and security, life and death, masculinity and femininity, and the love-hate inherent in the original triangle relationship of parents and child—rather than about world events or major issues. "A dream is a personal document, a letter to oneself. It is not a newspaper story or magazine article." In that letter to oneself, then, is revealed how the person truly sees himself when he has stripped off his waking pretenses, how he sees the people and pressures of his environment, how he perceives his impulses and wishes and the moral conflicts they so often create. Everything in the dream, says Hall, is our own creation and thus we are responsible for it. But our dream pictures, he warns, only show us our subjective reality; that is, they tell us how we feel about things, not how they actually are.

Hall warns that analyzing just one dream and drawing conclusions from it can be misleading. Only by studying a series of dreams, each related to the other "like the chapters of a novel," can we gain useful insight into our underlying conflicts and our ways of viewing the world that may not have been apparent in waking life.

. . . And How We Dream It. Dreams speak to us in another language—the language of parables, allegory, poetry, paradox, and, above all, symbols. Why do dreams speak to us in symbols, in pictorial metaphors, rather than directly? Contrary to what Freud thought, symbols have no intention of deceiving us; they are, in fact, getting through to us in the strongest way possible. Symbols are so powerfully charged with psychic energy—the same energy with which primitive man once endowed his world, and which we are all the poorer for having lost in modern civilization—that we are forced to pay attention to them. When we dream of careening wildly in a driverless car, it's easy to realize that we are out of control; when we dream of tidal waves engulfing us, we know that our emotions are overwhelming us; when we dream of ourselves in old, outdated clothes, we can see that our attitudes need some updating. Long lectures on the same subjects could scarcely have the same impact.

Nor is it always necessary to translate a symbol literally. Just as important is tuning in on the emotional content behind the symbol, asking ourselves how it makes us feel. As we do this, we find that symbols can provide us with their own consciousness-transforming energy, moving us always into new spaces from which we can grow and change.

Despite the fact that you can look up the meanings of symbols in dozens of dream dictionaries, it is important to remember that each symbol means something unique for you, depending on your personal associations and life experiences. True, there are general and universal symbols (some of which you can begin to work with on page 12) that can be used as touchstones to personal interpretations. But the important dream dictionary is the one you will compile yourself, after you have worked with your dreams for some time. Remember, too, that the richer your associations, the more you study all kinds of symbols from many cultures—ancient, mythic, modern—the more they will appear in your dream life and enrich your waking consciousness.

Act II: How to Help Your Dreams Help You

Recalling Your Dreams. We know from laboratory research that there is no such person as a non-dreamer. But we also know that dreams are slippery, mercurial, jealous of being captured; a strategy is necessary. Here, then, are some hints to help you work out your own system—your own ritual, in effect—for getting hold of your dreams.

First. Formulate a clear intention that you will remember your dreams; repeat this intention frequently during the day, and particularly before going to sleep. But remember that the unconscious responds to loving suggestion more gracefully than to command. Become a fisherman of the unconscious, surprising dreams into your net. Let the dreamer within know that you value it and will work with its messages.

Second. Get yourself in a relaxed state before going to sleep, by whatever physical or mental technique that works for you. Avoid sleeping pills; they lessen REM activity. Some people find that reviewing the events of the day backwards before they drift off helps dream recall. Henry Reed, the editor of the *Sundance Community Dream Journal*, suggests the Tibetan technique of focusing the desire for dreams into a concentrated "glow" in the back of the throat. One psychiatrist advises taking Vitamin B6, while Amanda Tree, a New York herbalist, claims that sleeping on a pillow stuffed with mugwort, yarrow and Foti-tieng increases dream recall. Don't worry if you do not dream; overwork, fatigue or other pressures can cause a temporary dry spell. If necessary, dream up a waking fantasy—and then proceed to work as if you had had an actual dream.

Third. Whenever you wake up from a dream—possibly during the night and certainly in the early morning—be ready to record your dreams, either in a note pad kept at your bedside, or in a tape recorder; the latter, a personal preference, takes less effort and is less disruptive of the feeling tone you are trying to recapture. Stay in one position until you have exhausted all your dream memories; then move gently into another sleeping position, and see if you can get more recall. Keeping your eyes closed, if possible, record your dreams in the present tense, noting first any dream poems or songs (the most fragile of dream memories), staying non-judgmental, and including even the most trivial or absurd-seeming fragments—they may be the very keys that will later unlock the dream's meaning. A morning meditation may bring back forgotten scenes, as will the day's waking activities.

Fourth. Transcribe your dream later in the day in your permanent dream diary, making it as beautiful as you can. Write the date, the number of the dream, and give it a title. Save space to draw dream pictures if you like, write your associations (see below), and make any comments—what may have taken place the day before that you connect with the dream, whatever your feelings about it may be. The dream is now fixed in permanent form so that you can work on it at your leisure. You will find this record especially valuable later when you study a series of your dreams, perhaps cross-referencing certain key categories. During the rest of the day, share your dream or ruminate on it alone, and see what new memories or insights arise. And be sure to thank your dreams for coming to you. The more you establish a friendly interaction with them, the more readily will they appear the next night. (See The Dream Diary, page 14.)

Incubating a Dream. Throughout history dreams have provided solutions for problems, affected healings, inspired artistic, creative, and scientific work on every level. Reporting to a scientific convention in 1890 on how he had finally succeeded in solving the long-baffling problem of the structure of the benzine ring—by inspiration received in a dream—Friedrich A. Kekule,

the German scientist, concluded his remarks with, "Let us learn to dream, gentlemen, and then we may perhaps find the truth." But we need not wait until dreams come to us when we have need of them; we can learn how to incubate or induce the very dreams we need, once we have mastered the art of dream recall. Only a few more steps need be added to those you have just learned. First: substitute the intention to have a specific kind of dream for the intention to recall a dream, and keep affirming it throughout the day. Second: begin with a question of modest proportions; prove the effectiveness of the method to yourself before you tackle the major problems of your life. Third: write out the problem fully before going to sleep. Ann Faraday, one of the pioneers of modern dream study, offers a wealth of practical suggestions for incubating dreams in *The Dream Game.* Kay C. Greene, a highly respected dream educator in New York City, suggests writing a letter to yourself stating all aspects of the problem and then putting it under your pillow and sleeping on it. Gayle Delaney, writing in the *Sundance Community Dream Journal,* advocates writing out a similar "incubation discussion," then listening "to the heart for a one-liner phrase or question that is a terse distillation of the incubation issue. . . . the dreamer must hold the incubation phrase clearly in mind, like a mantra, focusing on only the phrase while passing into sleep." If, for any reason, you fail to get the dream or do not understand its message, ask that it be repeated the next night; it usually will be, and often in a clearer form. Continue asking, if necessary. Patience, as in all aspects of dream work, is essential here. (See The Dream Bridge, page 32, for another exercise in incubating dreams.)

Interacting with Your Dreams. Now you're ready to begin constructing your own maps of the dream universe, to interact with your dreams. Notice that we use the work "interact" in a larger sense than merely "interpret," since a dream need not be translated literally—just as

a poem or painting need not be—in order to affect you. Working with dreams in the ways we suggest, you will be tapping into your own inner life, discovering wellsprings of energy, creativity, and insight you may have scarcely suspected.

Some ground rules to begin. Never give a dream a preconceived meaning; let it speak for itself. In the ancient world, a dream was interpreted solely according to the associations of the interpreter. Freud used the patient's associations, but gave *his* interpretation. Our aim is to show you how to interact with a dream so that it interprets itself. Avoid labeling dreams as either "good" or "bad"—all are valuable for lesson-learning. Finally, never let anyone impose a meaning upon your dream, although another person can be very helpful in guiding you to the point where you can see it for yourself. When an interpretation rings a deep bell within you, you will know it is right.

Associating to a Dream. Ann Faraday is known for a three-stage method of dream interpretation that is very fruitful. (See her books, *Dream Power* and *The Dream Game* for an extensive treatment.) Looking at your dream, ask yourself first if it speaks to you directly. Is it giving you a practical message about something in your real world that needs attending to? (If, for example, you dream that you have trouble braking your car, get it over to a mechanic before you start analyzing whether your emotions are out of control or you're driving too fast on the highway of life. Dreams have a way of picking up subliminal bits of information and alerting us to practical matters.) If there is no such message, then look for the dream's symbolic meaning; most likely it is dealing with something on an emotional level. The next step is to associate to its key words, phrases and symbols. Write them down, then choose any of the following techniques, or combinations of techniques, that seem workable.

Suppose one of your dream symbols is "baby." If you choose to work with *direct association*, give all of your ideas directly connected with baby; for example, "a baby is a small human creature, warm, cuddly, needing lots of care and love." Using *free association*, instead, you would simply associate off the top of your head on the word "baby," writing down whatever wild thoughts occur; for example, "baby . . . mother . . . hospital . . . crib . . . stuck . . . helpless . . . alone." (Try working with an idea like this in a group, and see how many different responses the same word will evoke!) If you still need to go deeper, try some *Jungian elaborations*, writing down everything you know about the purpose, construction, and function of babies. Now, write a story connecting all the symbols. As you will readily see, working with symbols releases some of their psychic energy, their emotional content, and allows you to enter into the dream on a feeling level. The dream then "interprets" itself. (See The Dream Association Tree, page 29.)

Gestalting a Dream. Another potent way to get in touch with the emotional reality of a dream is to "gestalt" it, or act it out. Working on the theory of Fritz Perls (see above) that every dream character or object—even a chair or a stove—stands for part of the dreamer's own self, you enact the dream from the point of view of each of the dream images. When two images clash, the dreamer has usually tuned in to the "topdog-underdog" aspects, the bullying-submissive aspects of the personality which hold each other perpetually in an unconscious tug of war. Through the encounter that follows—usually highly charged with emotion—a resolution is reached. A second person as guide can be helpful in directing the conversation and asking questions of the images. Classically, the subject sits in one chair (the "hot seat") and then another, switching back and forth, to move more readily into the bodily "set" of each particular character. The simplicity of the method belies its enormous power for release and transformation. Com-

The Search

The Game

menting on a dream which she had ge
stalted in one of Kay Greene's Dream
Workshops in New York City, a young
woman reported to me: "I knew the
dream was important when I had it, but
I couldn't look at it until I was forced to
confront the elements of the dream and
get into its meaning. The dialogue
(which continued in my head for several
hours after the session) came like a
series of doors that you can go through.
You go through one door, and then you
find that other doors open. You just
keep tearing the dream apart in your
mind, and each time you go through
another door and come out in a deeper
place."

Creative Writing Around a Dream. Instead of acting out your dream, try writing the dialogue of each character. Write it as a play; or write a letter from one image to another. You will be astounded at the answers you get back! Even those who feel they have no ability at writing have been amazed at the intensity of feeling this approach can unleash.

Many different writing approaches will suggest themselves as you continue to work with dreams. You might, for example, rewrite the endings of your dreams. (See Dream-It-Yourself Comics, page 16.) You can write titles, themes, and morals for all of your dreams; when you have collected a series of dreams, construct stories from each of these elements. As you're writing, focus on what moved you most in the dream; ask yourself if you were afraid of anything in the dream, or if you'd like to have that dream again. If a dream image troubles you, challenge it to explain itself. (See Unmasking the Dream Demons, page 21.) Make up new ways to create stories, poems, fantasies; the more you continue to work this way, the more the dreamer within will feed you material.

Drawing Your Dream. A fourth major way to interact with your dreams is through the medium of graphic art, which uses the same kinds of forms and symbols that a dream does. When we draw our dreams we are recreating them directly, without the necessity of translating them into the new language of words. (See The Dream Mandala, page 30; also try making the kind of dream collages that appear throughout this book.) One of the best ways to help children who have frightening dreams is to hand them crayons or paints or clay and say, "Show me how you felt in the dream."

No matter which creative process you choose—acting, writing, drawing—you will find an amazing thing happening: a point will inevitably come when the images from the unconscious take over and do the creating. When this happens, you know that you have reached a new level of communication with the dreamer within. As the dream images take on their own life and seek their own expression, you have entered not only into the heart of the dream, but into the heart of the artistic process itself.

Dream Groups. All of these techniques can be done individually or, better still, in a dream group. (We are presuming that those with serious emotional problems will work on their dreams under the guidance of a psychotherapist.) If you don't have a dream group—start one! Two people working together for a while can generate a climate of enthusiasm that can lead to three, and three to four and more. None of you need be experts; your dreams will be your teacher. For guidance and inspiration in working with leaderless groups, see the *Sundance Community Dream Journal* (especially Volume 1, No. 2).

Act III: Changing Your Dreams to Change Your Life

After you have worked with dreams for some time and felt their power, you may be ready for the postgraduate course: changing the contents of dreams—modifying behavior, so to speak, right in the dream state—and, by so doing, making changes in your waking behavior that go far beyond what you had imagined possible before. Whether intentional direction of the dream state is desirable or not is much debated currently. Some warn that to condition our dreams is just another form of manipulation, one that will do violence to our inner nature. Others, however, claim that everything that we see, think, feel, and do has already conditioned the dream state; why not, then, influence it in a positive direction for positive results?

How is it possible that a dream can be conditioned? The reason that the dream state is so malleable, so plastic, is that ordinary dreaming has no central reference point. Give the unconscious a reference point, however, and it immediately starts producing the kind of dreams you desire. As James L. Donohoe writes in *Dream Reality:* "Dream structure will shift to accommodate the assumptions and expectations of the dreamer. Changing these assumptions is the key to working consciously with the dream state."

Senoi Dreaming. Perhaps the best example of a dream-control system that works is found among the Senois, a primitive tribe living in the jungles of Malaysia, whose idyllic society, free of war, violence, physical and mental illness, is largely based on the knowledge received from dreams. Harmonious, artistically creative, and highly cooperative people, the Senois train their youngsters from earliest childhood in the appropriate ways to dream. Can this system of dream control have any meaning for those of us who live in the jungle of modern civilization? Patricia Garfield, whose book *Creative Dreaming* presents the best popular treatment of the Senois (and of intentional dreaming in general), thinks there is much we can learn from Senoi dreamers.

The Senois consider everyone they meet in their dreams to be a part of their own selves. According to Garfield (whose highly detailed instructions for applying the Senoi principles in your own life are well worth studying), their major teaching is to confront and conquer danger in the dream. If an enemy attacks or threatens you, you must fight it, either alone or with the help of dream friends. After you have subdued it, you must obtain a gift from it to bring back to your people. Should you kill the enemy, it is reborn as comrade and ally. Translated into psychological terms, we must be willing to confront and accept those things we dislike and fear in ourselves, overcome them, and extract their positive essence. Until we can separate ourselves from those unwanted aspects of our personality and move out of an unconscious relationship with them into a direct encounter, we cannot move ahead. A further psychological parallel: the Senoi idea of extracting a gift from a defeated enemy or a lover, and then re-creating it—by means of a poem, story, song or painting—corresponds precisely with the Jungian idea of working with the creative products of dream inspiration to deepen the process of individuation.

Two other Senoi principles are important: always advance toward pleasure in a dream, and achieve a positive outcome. If you dream of a sexual adventure, let it reach its climax; if you dream of falling, convert the fear of falling into the exhilaration of flying. The benefits of applying Senoi principles are far-reaching, says Garfield. They can "reorganize the dreamer's internal experience in such a way that his personality becomes unified. The results of an unpleasant experience in waking life are at first neutralized in his dreams, then reversed. Negative images, if they occur at all, are no longer frightening: tension is reduced. The energy that went into forming negative images is transformed into a positive creative product." In other words, the dialogue between the conscious and the unconscious has been transformed.

Even if you do not deliberately program yourself to have Senoi-type dreams, you may find that simply knowing about them can change your dream life. This is what happened to me when, after immersing myself in Senoi concepts, I dreamed one night of three huge lions slowly materializing on a mountain path and blocking my way down the road. Choosing not to escape by an alternate path, as others were doing, and facing the lions instead, I saw them first disappear, only to immediately reappear in my living room, squeezing their way through the cracks in the front door. As my family watched in the background, I found myself, normally a champion coward, taking charge. "In the name of Sai Baba, I order you to dissolve," I shouted at them. "In the name of Sai Baba, I order you to dissolve!" (Sai Baba is an Indian sage who had become my dream ally.) To my amazement, the lions did exactly that, and I awoke with a great feeling of victory. A few days later, walking into a store, I found a huge dog—the kind that would ordinarily frighten me—directly in my path. Sensing that my dream might, in a sense, be coming true and wondering if, indeed, Senoi dream confrontation could enable one to overcome phobias and fear patterns, I found that my real-life fear vanished in seconds; I stepped calmly around the dog and even smiled at him. From my own admittedly limited experience, I should have to agree with Garfield's contention that "the Senoi system may provide us with the means to deal with a person's fears where they originate, in his own mind, instead of years later with a therapist. . . . After you have successfully dealt with your enemies in the dream world, it suddenly becomes easier to deal with threat in the waking world." The "gift" I had extracted from my dream was courage.

Lucid Dreaming. In Senoi dreaming, one has a semi-conscious awareness of the dream state. In the lucid dream, however, which is perhaps the highest form of intentional dreaming, the dreamer moves on to a new level of consciousness, in which he maintains the awareness of the waking ego while still in the environment of the dream state. This is the dream theater at its highest

level. The dreamer who knows that he is dreaming is no longer subject to the vagaries of an involuntary experience; he has the power to change the contents of his dream at will. The possibilities of this kind of dream control are mind-boggling. In a lucid dream one may ask for and receive solutions to problems; converse with great people; read dream manuscripts; hear dream music; visit dream museums; intensify the colors or change the scenery of the dream landscape in any way one likes; fly to strange and wonderful places; have telepathic and clairvoyant experiences; defy every law of time and space. On a therapeutic level, knowing that one is merely dreaming and cannot be hurt, one can resolve nightmares and encourage positive experiences. Anything that a person can hope to achieve in the course of incubating dreams and patiently waiting for answers can be done instantly if he or she becomes a lucid dreamer.

On a still deeper level, lucid dreaming can take one into the highest stages of altered consciousness. Comparing lucid dreaming to the Tibetan Yogic practice of entering the dreaming state in full consciousness so that one can realize that the waking state is also a self-created dream, G. Scott Sparrow writes in *Lucid Dreaming*: ". . . this recognition leads the adept to the second and most important phase of the lucid dream, which is meditating on the Reality behind the dream images. Thus the lucid dreamer enters into an illumined state which in the Tibetan text is known as the 'Dawning of the Clear Light.'"

While Patricia Garfield in *Creative Dreaming* shows how to train oneself to become a lucid dreamer—by picking up cues as to when elements in a dream appear incongruous, by cultivating dreams of flying (these often precede lucid experiences), and by many other programming techniques—other dream educators believe that lucid dreaming need not be deliberately sought for but will develop naturally after one has spent a long time working with dreams to clear up his life prob-

lems. G. Scott Sparrow suggests meditating in the early hours of the morning (somewhere between 3:00 and 4:00 A.M.), and then going back to sleep as a method of attunement that may produce lucidity. (My own personal experience has been that the early morning meditation is effective.) I am inclined to believe, however, that working too hard—straining for a lucid dream, or any kind of dream experience for that matter—is self-defeating. The special dream experiences will come in their own good time if we are receptive to them; the unconscious needs its own time to bear its fruits. As James Donohoe writes in *Dream Reality*: "To approach the cultivation of inner abilities in a very structured and goal-directed way invites failure. Even with success, the main point has been missed; that of the joy and boundary-surpassing nature of inner exploration. . . . the intuitive is more a matter for the poet than for the technician."

Epilogue: How to Use This Book

The exercises that follow have been designed to take you step by step into the dream experience. We suggest, therefore, that you familiarize yourself with all of them, then work on them in the order in which they appear in the book. You will want to tear out certain pages; fill in other pages; copy or duplicate some so that you can work with them again. Then, adding your own dream records, you can make this book as large as you wish, and thus create your first notebook of dreams.

And now the stage has been set for your own dream adventures. We invite you to enter the magic world of the dream theater.

The Language of Dreams
(What Symbols Can Mean)

Dreams speak to us in a language that we have always known—even though we are yet to learn it consciously. Picture language is perhaps the most ancient language, coming from the deepest strata of the mind. That is why it can so powerfully influence us; dreams, after all, do not bother coming to us to tell us something we already know. The dreamer within likes to create puns, associating similar ideas simply because the words for them sound the same.

For example, he may show you a picture of a school of fish when he is suggesting you need some more schooling. Always stay open to the meaning of dreams, because below the surface level of humor there is always a serious intent.

Activity. Below the picture, we have suggested some possible meanings for these puns. Before you look at them, write down your personal associations and see how they compare. Then make up some dreamy puns of your own.

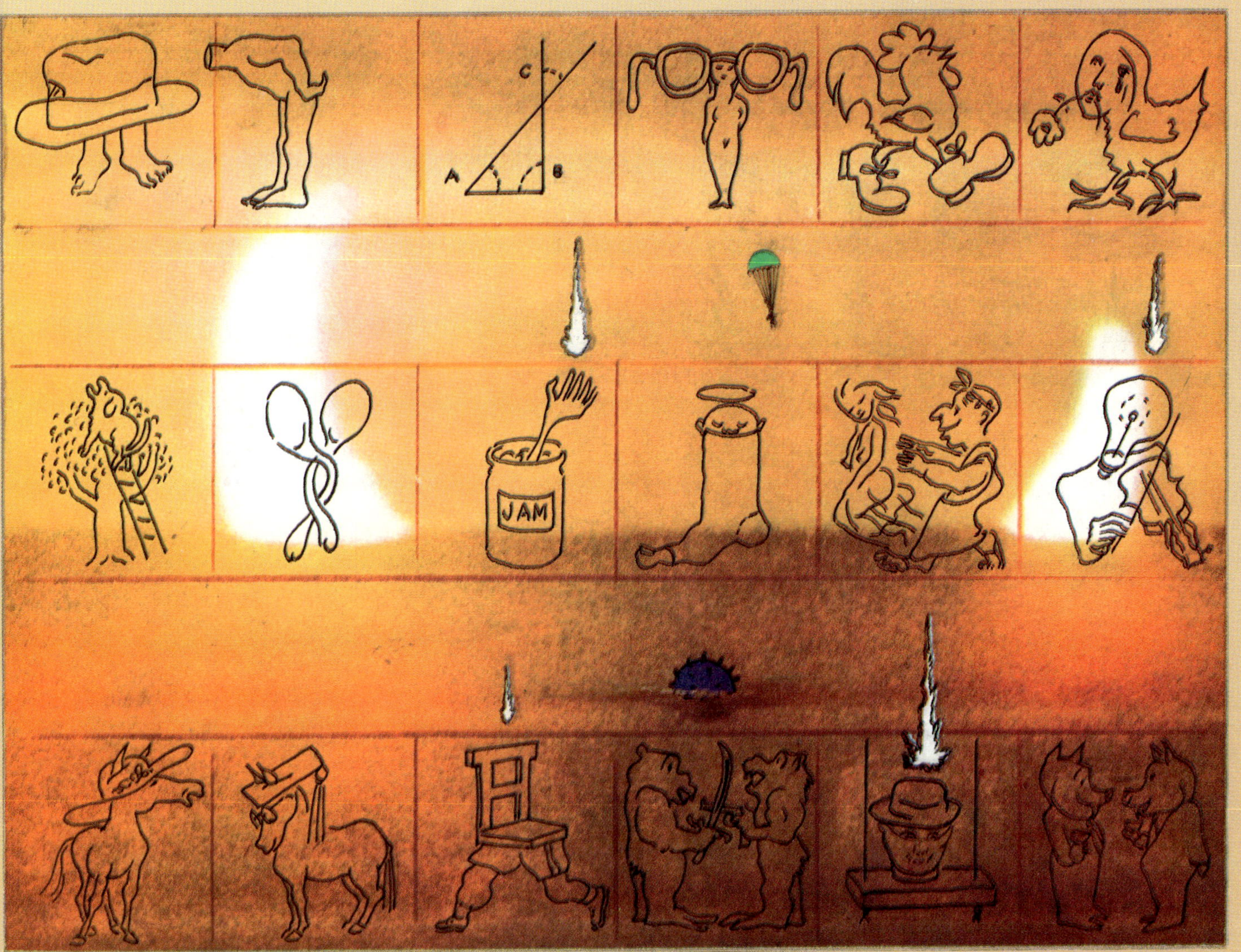

- Keep it under your hat
- Losing your head
- A new angle
- Don't make a spectacle of yourself
- Cock o' the walk
- She's no spring chicken
- Barking up a tree
- Spooning
- In a jam
- Holy
- Julius Caesar
- A sound idea
- Don't nag
- Horse sense
- You need to be jogged
- Guerilla warfare
- Taking a swing
- A boring talk

As you begin to work with your dreams, you will find many symbols—of a more abstract nature than those shown on the previous page—beginning to appear. Shown below is a "dream dictionary" of universal symbols and their general meanings—which will also have specific meanings for each and every dreamer.

Activity. Using these symbols as memory joggers, start to compile your Dream Calendar (opposite page). Begin, if possible, on a quiet weekend, when you will be relaxed and more likely to recall your dreams. Cut out and paste these symbols in the appropriate boxes, adding your own drawings or words as you wish. You will already have begun to paint your own dream pictures, and will be ready for the more detailed work on the next page.

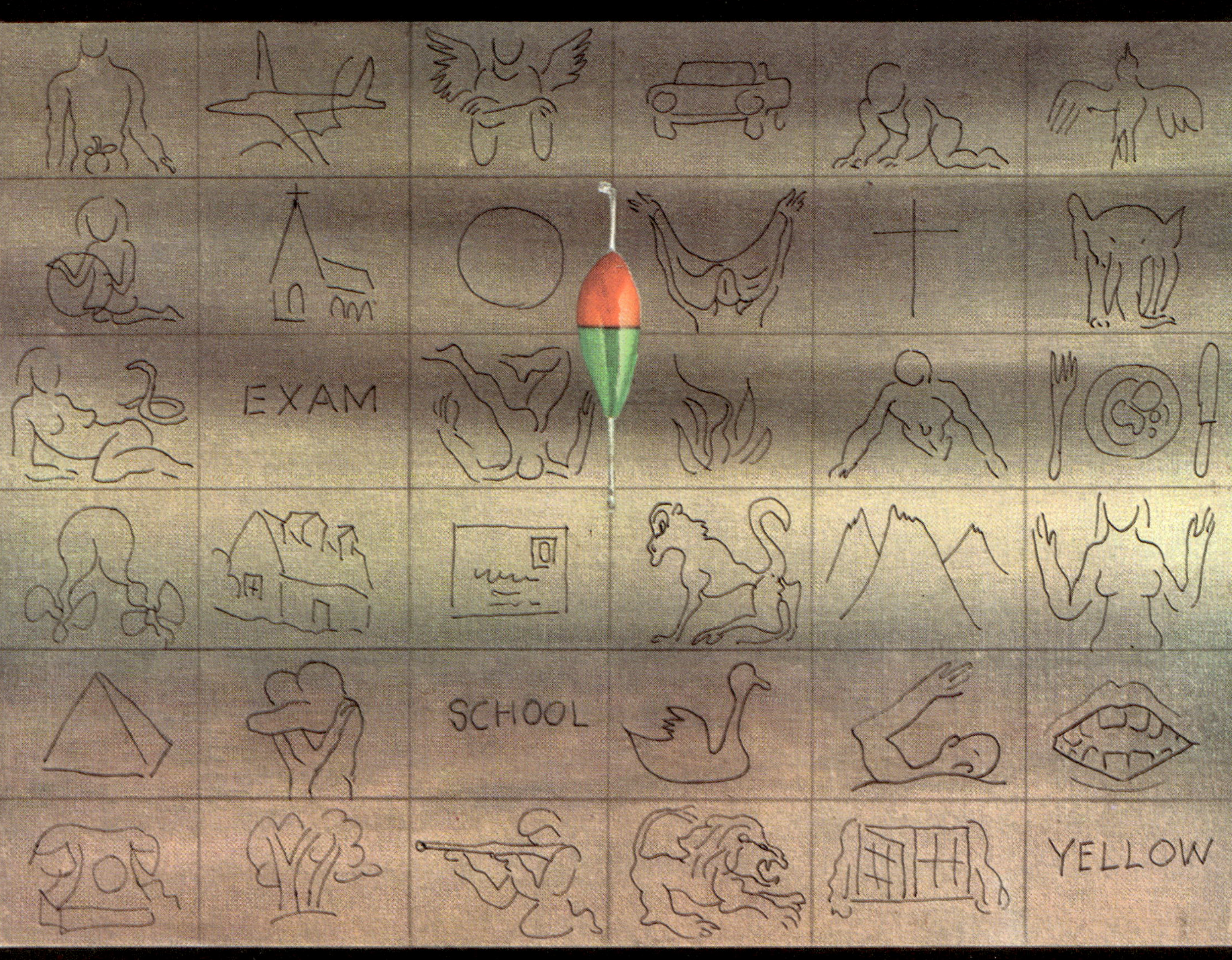

1.	Adam	Instinctive man, nature, strength
2.	Airplane	Physical body, spiritual attitudes
3.	Angel	Higher self, source of help
4.	Automobile	Ambition or drive, physical body
5.	Baby	Brain child, innocence
6.	Bird	Freedom, the soul
7.	Child	Rebirth, inspiration, guide
8.	Church	Spiritual life, moral ideals
9.	Circle	Wholeness, integration, eternity
10.	Clothes	Attitudes, disguises
11.	Cross	Power of protection, difficulty, unity
12.	Elephant	Wisdom, strength, obstacles removed
13.	Eve	*Anima* figure, temptress, nature
14.	Examination	Life test, fear of failing
15.	Falling	Out of control, headed for a fall
16.	Fire	Purification, destruction, passion
17.	Flying	Overcoming, pride, sex
18.	Food	Security, sustenance, gluttony
19.	Hair	Thoughts, sensuality
20.	House	Your life, areas of the psyche
21.	Letter	Information about yourself or others
22.	Monkey	Trickster, instinctive energy
23.	Mountains	Obstacles, spiritual achievement
24.	Nudity	Vulnerability, hiding nothing
25.	Pyramid	Initiation, rising of spiritual power
26.	Sex	Integration, union, aggression
27.	School	The lessons of life
28.	Swan	The spirit, solitary grace, pride
29.	Swimming	At ease with the subconscious
30.	Teeth (loss of)	Loss of power, loose talk
31.	Telephone	Inner messages, communication
32.	Tree	Aspiration, development, fruitfulness
33.	War	Internal conflict, strife
34.	Wild Animals	Pursuit, denied instinctive drives
35.	Window	Perspective, an opening
36.	Yellow	Cowardly, sunny

Your Dream Calendar

SATURDAY	SUNDAY	MONDAY	TUESDAY
WEDNESDAY	THURSDAY	FRIDAY	SATURDAY
SUNDAY	MONDAY	TUESDAY	WEDNESDAY
THURSDAY	FRIDAY	SATURDAY	SUNDAY

The Dream Diary
(Remembering and Beginning to Understand Your Dreams)

Now you're ready for the most important single step in working with dreams: keeping a dream diary. The page below is a sample of how you should set up your own dream notebook.

Activity. Following the suggestions given on page 5/6 record the date and number of the dream, and give it a

Dream No. 1   Date

Dream No. 2   Date

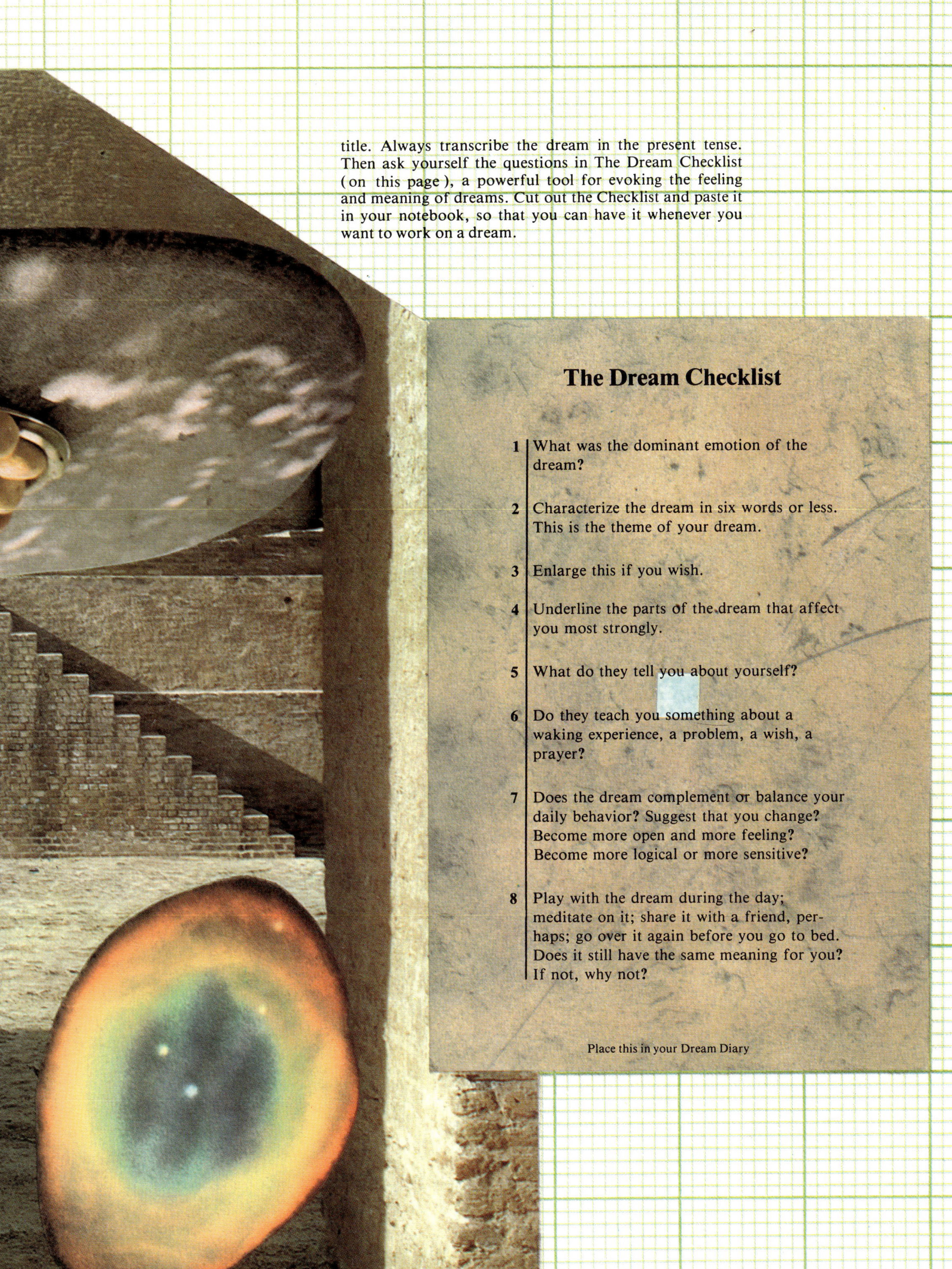

title. Always transcribe the dream in the present tense. Then ask yourself the questions in The Dream Checklist (on this page), a powerful tool for evoking the feeling and meaning of dreams. Cut out the Checklist and paste it in your notebook, so that you can have it whenever you want to work on a dream.

The Dream Checklist

1 What was the dominant emotion of the dream?

2 Characterize the dream in six words or less. This is the theme of your dream.

3 Enlarge this if you wish.

4 Underline the parts of the dream that affect you most strongly.

5 What do they tell you about yourself?

6 Do they teach you something about a waking experience, a problem, a wish, a prayer?

7 Does the dream complement or balance your daily behavior? Suggest that you change? Become more open and more feeling? Become more logical or more sensitive?

8 Play with the dream during the day; meditate on it; share it with a friend, perhaps; go over it again before you go to bed. Does it still have the same meaning for you? If not, why not?

Place this in your Dream Diary

Dream-It-Yourself Comics
(Re-experiencing Your Dreams)

A dynamic way to interact with your dreams is to change the script. If you don't like the ending of a dream—or even if you do—experiment with changing it. By doing so, you are breaking down the barriers between dream life and waking fantasy, so that you move into a creative partnership with the dreamer within. Eventually, you may be able to achieve the state of lucid dreaming. When this happens you are aware that you are dreaming and can change

Original Dream

1. I am walking naked down the main street. 2. A police car pulls up. 3. The cop shouts at me. 4. And I am frightened.

Re-creation

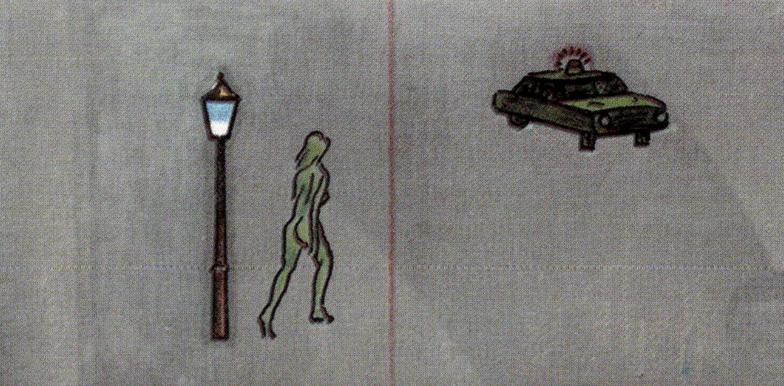
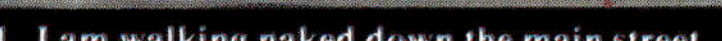

1. I am walking naked down the main street. 2. The policeman shouts at me. 3. I don my Superwoman cloak and start to fly. 4. Everybody gasps.

Original Dream

1. I visit the Zoo and find all the cages empty. 2. I feel afraid. 3. And look for a way to protect myself. 4. So I lock myself in.

Re-creation

the scenario in the very act of dreaming it.

Activity. After studying the first example of changing a dream, proceed to either draw, write, make a collage, cut out your photo, or work in any way that occurs to you, in order to refashion the next two dream comics so that you like the endings better. Use the two blank strips to work with a dream of your own. First record the dream as it was; then recreate it in a new way.

Original Dream

1. A beautiful woman takes me to a magic island.
2. Where we spend the night.
3. The next morning, I am alone.
4. And the island is slowly sinking.

Re-creation

Your Original Dream

Re-creation

The Dream Personality Workshop
(Meeting Your Many Selves)

In the dream world, we meet parts of ourselves that we have alienated in our waking lives. What we do not acknowledge in ourselves, we project on and often resent in others. By becoming open to these unrecognized aspects of ourselves and acknowledging them, we can let the dream teach us to be whole.

Activity. Cut out a small photograph of your head, and place it on each of these archetypal figures, ignoring factors of age and sex (the psyche is both old and young, masculine and feminine). Then, use the emotional reaction sheet for each one; by evoking these feeling responses, you can bypass the intellect, going straight to the heart.

Emotional Reaction Sheet

1. First reaction (one word). _______________

2. You feel ☐ exhilarated ☐ comfortable ☐ passive ☐ confused ☐ authoritative ☐ silly ☐ disgusted ☐ frightened ☐ stupid ☐ balanced ☐ whole. _______

3. What are the first words you would say as this personality? _______________

4. What is the first action you would take as this personality? _______________

5. Write a dream as each personality. _______________

6. Would you want to remember this dream? _______________

7. How would you feel on awaking after this dream? _______________

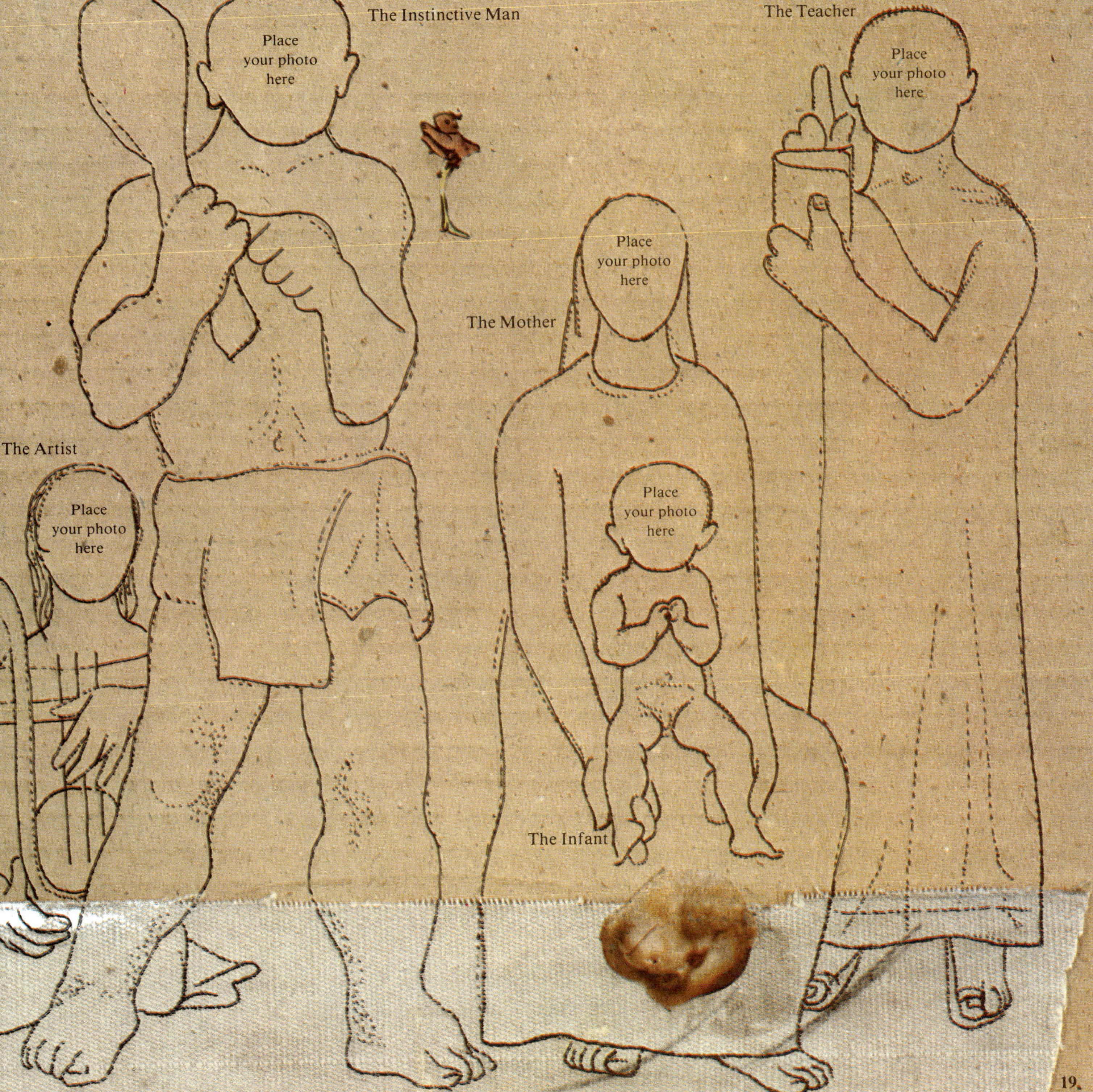

The Instinctive Man
The Teacher
Place your photo here
Place your photo here
The Mother
Place your photo here
The Artist
Place your photo here
Place your photo here
The Infant

The Dream Demons Unmasked

(A Call for Help from the Unknown You)

Dreams are not always pleasant. We have all experienced nightmares from which we wake in terror and try as quickly as we can to wipe out of our minds. But such dreams are often the most important of all, the ones we can least afford to ignore. Since dreams function in a compensatory way, restoring our psychological equilibrium, we can see that a nightmare shows us precisely what part of ourselves we have alienated or disowned. In the form of a dream image, it can surface when we least expect it, treating us with equal justice as we have treated it—but now it is a "dream demon," grown hideous by suppression.

A simplified example will show how dream demons are created. Suppose that a middle-aged man dreams of a ferocious giant, ugly, grotesque, with a sailor's tattoo on his left arm. Clawing apart the bars of a cage in which he has been imprisoned, the giant lunges toward the man and lays his huge hands around his throat. The man wakes up, choking and gasping. In order to understand what caused this dream, let's look upon it as Act II of a play in the Dream Theater. Act I occurred in the man's real life, some time back. As a young man, he had wanted to run away to sea, but had squashed this impulse and instead accepted a tedious job that would allow him to stay at home and care for his invalid mother. But the adventurous sailor—that part of himself that he has repressed—had not been destroyed, merely cast into a psychic dungeon. Here, ignored by the dreamer's conscious mind, he has grown monstrous and is now clamoring to be free; indeed, if he is not freed, he will surely destroy the man.

By realizing this, by unmasking the monster and seeing that he is simply a part of himself that must be acknowledged, the dreamer can create a happy real-life Act III for himself. By changing his behavior to give this part of himself its natural expression, he thus transforms the demon into the life-giving energy that makes him whole.

But all dreams, obviously, are not as clear-cut as this one. How can we go about unmasking the demons of our dreams and using their energy for positive growth? In the dream state itself, we can practice the Senoi technique of consciously confronting and conquering our dream enemies (see page 9). If we can achieve lucid dreaming (see page 10) and thus change our dream environment at will, we can learn to harmonize with and forgive our negative dream images, as well as conquer them if necessary. But these techniques are for advanced dreamers; we can begin right now, in waking fantasies, to dispose of the demons. Once the dream lesson is learned, the nightmare ends. Following the technique of gestalting or acting out a dream (see page 7), let's engage the dream demon in a little dialogue.

Activity. Using one of your own nightmares as the basis, take alternating parts and fill in the blanks in the following conversation. Then reconstruct Act I of your dream scenario. You can use this procedure whenever you are confronted by a dream image—positive or negative—that you do not understand.

<table>
<tr><th>The Dreamer</th><th>The Demon</th></tr>
<tr><td>Dreamer. "What do you want from me?"</td><td>Demon. "________________________"</td></tr>
<tr><td>Dreamer. "But why do you have to be so terrifying about it?"</td><td>Demon. "________________________
________________________"</td></tr>
<tr><td>Dreamer. "What do you mean, I never pay attention?"</td><td>Demon. "________________________"</td></tr>
<tr><td>Dreamer. "You mean it's been going on for as long as that?"</td><td>Demon. "________________________
________________________"</td></tr>
<tr><td>Dreamer. "But what did I ever do to hurt you?"</td><td>Demon. "Even if I told you, you'd never admit it anyway, right?"</td></tr>
<tr><td>Dreamer. "________________________
________________________"</td><td>Demon. "But do you really see what it means?"</td></tr>
<tr><td>Dreamer. "________________________"</td><td>Demon. "Now you've got it."</td></tr>
<tr><td>Dreamer. "How can I make it up to you, then?"</td><td>Demon. "________________________"</td></tr>
<tr><td>Dreamer. "I need you. How can I change so that we can be friends?"</td><td>Demon. "________________________
________________________"</td></tr>
</table>

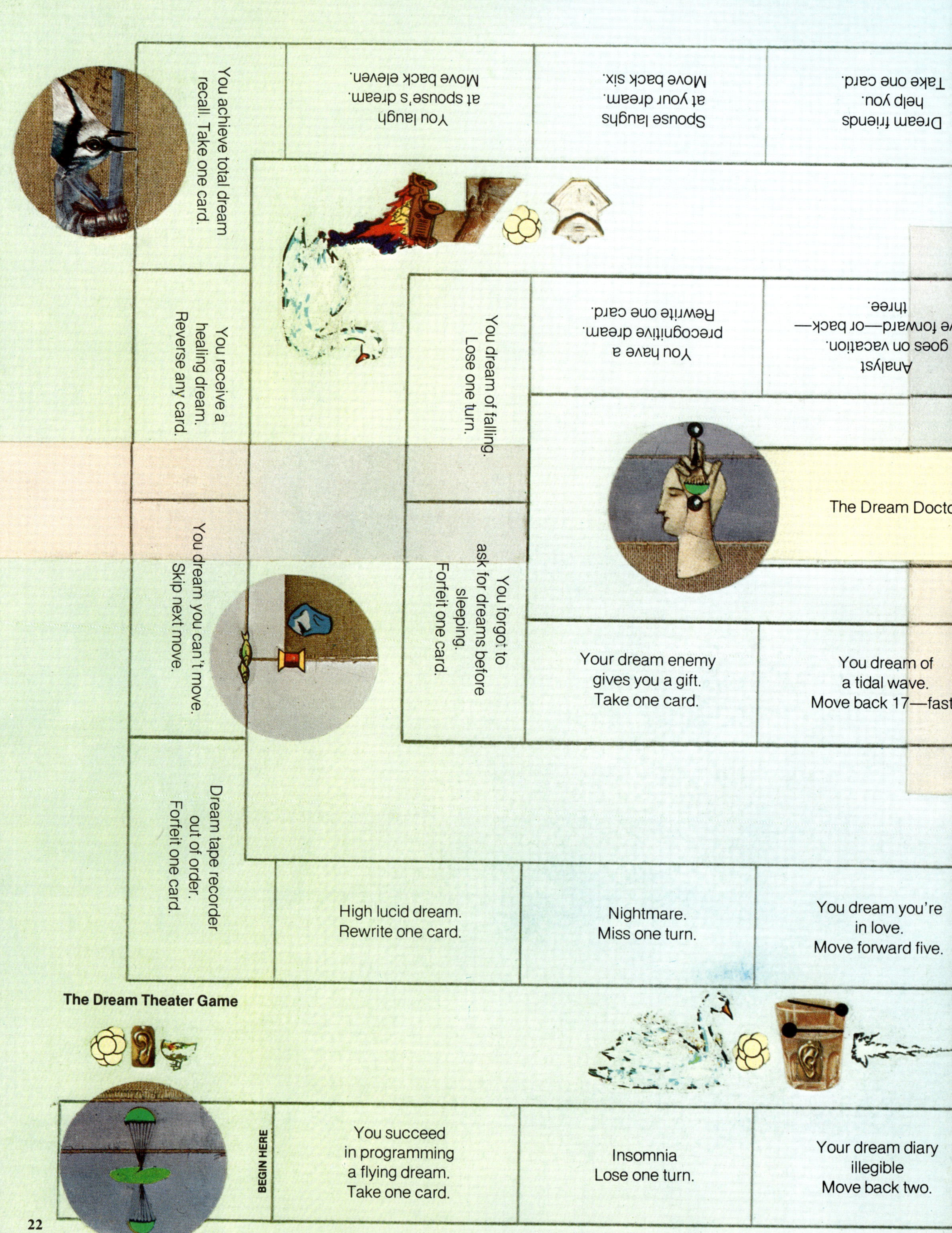

You achieve total dream recall. Take one card.
You laugh at spouse's dream. Move back eleven.
Spouse laughs at your dream. Move back six.
Dream friends help you. Take one card.
You receive a healing dream. Reverse any card.
You dream of falling. Lose one turn.
You have a precognitive dream. Rewrite one card.
Analyst goes on vacation. ...ve forward—or back—three.
The Dream Docto
You dream you can't move. Skip next move.
You forgot to ask for dreams before sleeping. Forfeit one card.
Your dream enemy gives you a gift. Take one card.
You dream of a tidal wave. Move back 17—fast
Dream tape recorder out of order. Forfeit one card.
High lucid dream. Rewrite one card.
Nightmare. Miss one turn.
You dream you're in love. Move forward five.
The Dream Theater Game
BEGIN HERE
You succeed in programming a flying dream. Take one card.
Insomnia Lose one turn.
Your dream diary illegible Move back two.

You dream of losing te...
Dentist out of town.
Lose one turn.

You forgot
and took sleeping pills.
Move back eight.

Meet dream guide.
Move forward six.

You hide a dream from your
analyst. Return last card.

You dream of
losing money.
Lose one turn.

Dream solves
a life problem.
Take one card

You analyze your dreams
while dreaming.
Reverse one card.

You are reborn
in dream
after being killed.
Take one card.

ream Waiting Room.
Move back
to original position.

Dream enemy
defeats you.
Lose two turns.

Dream dragon of self-doubt
eats you.
Go back to the beginning.

Dream incubation
succeeds.
Take one card.

Mediation improves
your dream life.
Take two cards.

Psychiatrist
doubles his fees.
Return one card
(or miss turn).

You dream at work.
Move back four.

You forgot to
ask for dreams
before sleeping.
Forfeit one card.

You succeed in
ESP dream experiment.
Take one card
from any player.

Anxiety dream.
Reverse last card.

elf-insight dream.
Take one card.

You dream you are
imprisoned in a dungeon.
Lose one turn.

Dream gives you
poem or song.
Take one card.

The Dream Theater Game Explained

You can play The Dream Theater Game anytime you wish, even before you have read the text of this book or tried any of the exercises. However, since one of the purposes of the game is to familiarize you with the basic teachings of dreams, it will have more meaning for you after you have read the book. Like a dream itself, a game calls up the intuition, the imagination, the spontaneous parts of ourselves and gives them equal status with the controlling mind. We play as we learn; we learn as we play.

Playing The Dream Theater game is, perhaps, a good way to start your own dream group where you will later work with more serious techniques (see page 9). Remember that at this point, the object is to have fun with your dreams; leave the serious depth probing to the professionals.

The Rules of the Game

The Dream Theater Game consists of two parts; in the first, a board game, players receive Dream Cards in the course of play; in the second, the Dream Cards are woven into personal dream stories by each player, and are read aloud and analyzed. Central to the game is the figure of The Dream Doctor, who is the first person to reach or pass the last square on the board, thus ending the first part of the game. Not only does he collect from each player a monetary fee agreed upon in advance—anything from 10¢ or more—but he has the right to give his interpretation of each player's dream.

The Play: Part I. The highest scorer on the throw of the dice goes first, and then the turn moves to the player on the right. As the game begins, two Dream Cards are dealt to each player from a shuffled pack; the remaining cards are then placed to one side of the board. As the game proceeds, players will land on squares which will either give or take away cards. (If, at any point, a player is requested to take cards and there are none remaining in the pack, he must move forward two spaces; if asked to return a card and he does not have one, he forfeits one turn.) Since the cards are printed on both sides, they must be used face up. If a player is asked to return a card, it is placed on the bottom of the deck. Each card is placed on a sheet of paper in front of the player as it is received. Once someone has become The Dream Doctor, board play ends and the first part of the game is over.

Part II. Now each player has five minutes in which to create his dream, weaving the cards—both words ánd pictures—together with his own story line. All the cards must be used, but they can be arranged in any order the player chooses. If a player has no cards, he must create an entire dream. (The player may write and read his dream, or simply improvise as he reads aloud.) After The Dream Doctor has interpreted his dream, the player is free to resist, disagree, argue, give his own interpretation—or even to agree. At this point, the kibitzers (the other players) are invited to join the free-for-all. Because of his elevated status, The Dream Doctor may share his dream or not, as he wishes. If the group agrees, each player may analyze the dream of one other player. If you wish, set a time limit—perhaps ten to fifteen minutes—for each interpretation and discussion.

Equipment: Included here are the Dream Board, which can be kept in the book, or torn out and mounted; and 32 Dream Cards, printed on each side, which must be torn out (pages 25 to 28). You should provide: dice, markers for each player, paper and pens. From 2 to 6 people can comfortably play.

A child gives
me
a golden spoon

"Your tax returns
are not in order,"
the executioner says

The centaur drinks
the champagne
and says . . . . .

Uncle Harry
is on
the television

Tomorrow
will be
officially
proclaimed

"I'll have
an orange souffle,"
says the waiter

My mother
serves me
an empty
soup plate

A blue rose
blooms
in the snow

"The bombs are
in the cupboard,"
says Mrs. Grimsby

I cannot
stop
the car

"Does anyone
wish to be
consecrated?"
asks the Bishop

My girl friend's
father
takes out
his knife

"You're going back
to outer space,"
my dog said,
weeping

The angel
says,
"Break your clay"

My bus
lets me off
in an unknown
neighborhood

A beautiful woman
awaits me in
the high tower

I am in
a boat with
no oars

An ambulance
arrives, and a
large policeman
is carried out
on a red stretcher

Menacing figures
are following me
They are carrying
a hammer,
a bow
and a black canary

I cannot find
the room where
the Latin examination
will be held

My kite
lifts me up
into
the elevator

A
blinding white
light
appears

I am naked
walking down
the main road

The train
approaches
the station
but will not
stop for me

A scream,
shrill
and terrible

The rainbow is
on
my pillow

The star
bursts into a
thousand fountains

I sit on
a stone
under a lake

The object
is obscured
by the
detective's shoe

The door opens,
revealing
a window

"You've won,"
said
the statue

"There's
no way out,
I'm afraid,"
she says

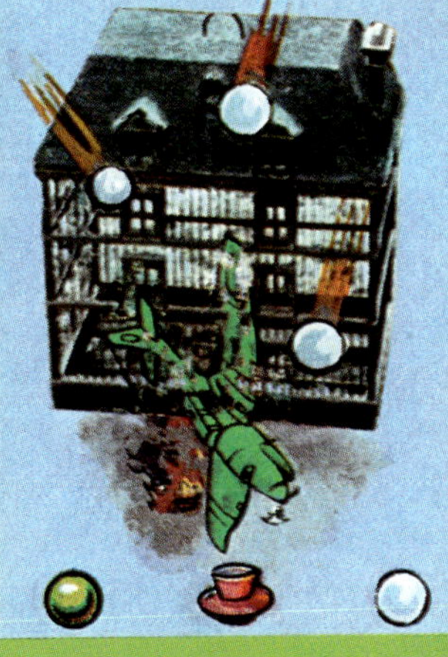

"I'd
like to be
your
Valentine."

At the foot
of the dark stairway
is a
locked door

"Congratulations,"
said the doctor
"You've given birth
to twins"

Fog
comes up
over
the land

The roof
catches fire
while I am
praying

The Marines
had scarcely landed
when the
bath attendant
appeared

I have space
to share with a
professional person

A sudden afternoon
thunderstorm
drops three inches
of snow on the
metropolitan area

"I've come for
your help,"
says the ghost

My suitcase
falls open and three
strange letters
fall to the ground

I
cannot move
my body

The great shark
stares at me

The gray man
sinks into
the gray mud

I meet
a man called
Mr. Success

I find gold
buried
in the snow

The clocks are
going backward

The Dream Association Tree
(Getting to the Roots of It All)

Associating to the symbols of a dream is the simplest and most direct way to approach it. (See page 6 for various association methods: direct association, free association, and Jungian elaboration).

Activity. Write your original dream in the top space.

In the four middle spaces, list all the key words, phrases, and proper names, and your associations to each of them. In the bottom space, link them together to form a new dream story. In this way, the seed of the dream flowers into new meaning.

Your Original Dream

Association Box

Association Box

Association Box

Association Box

Your New Dream

The Dream Mandala
(Centering the Self)

The mandala—Jung's "magic circle" which restores a lost sense of inner balance—has appeared in dreams and myths since primitive times. When one begins to dream of mandalas, he is putting the Self (of which the ego is only a part), at the center of his universe and relating it to the cosmos. The mandala is the symbol of wholeness, a visual representation of great force, whose harmonizing energy we can partake of—through dreaming of mandalas, draw-

ing them or meditating on them.

Activity. First: Choose those symbols whose qualities you need. Then paste them on the mandala on this page, hanging it where you can see it before dreaming. Second: Make mandalas using the symbols of your own dreams—either from one dream or from several. As you do so, more and more symbols will evolve and present themselves for you to work with.

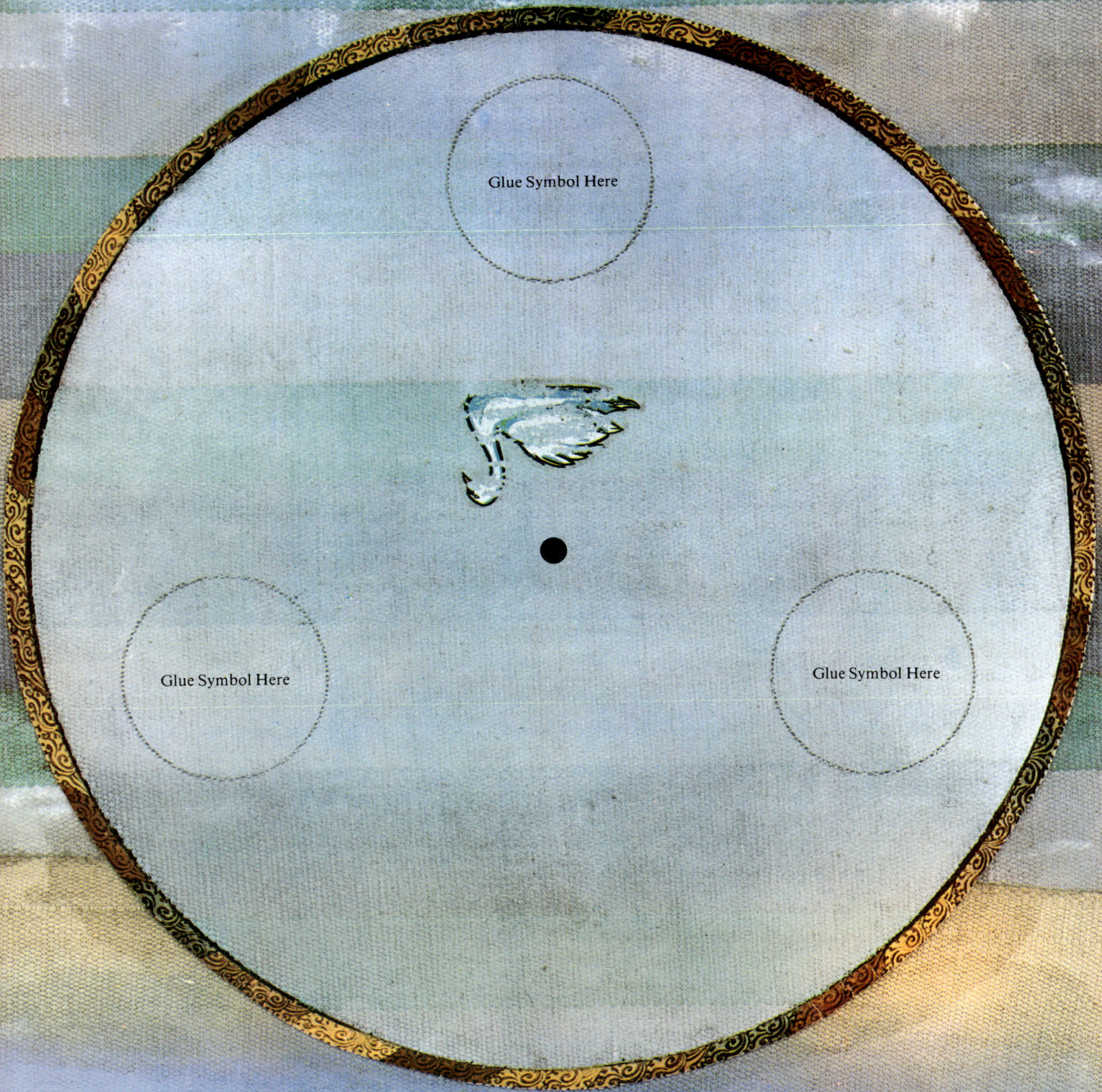

The Dream Bridge
(Dream Steps to a New You)

Once you have learned how to incubate specific dreams to solve specific problems (see page 6), you can use that technique to change aspects of your personality, with which you are not satisfied. If you are willing to follow the advice of the dreamer within and to take responsibility for its answers, you will be led, step by step, to the psychological foundation of the problem. Suppose, to take a simple example, a woman wishes to lose weight. Posing the problem to her dreams she would first ask, "Why am I fat?" When the answer comes through, she must take great care that it is valid; unless dreams lead the way, the process is simply self-suggestion. Suppose the answer of the dream is, "Because you're afraid of men." The dialogue continues through a series of nights. *Woman:* "Why am I afraid of men?" *Dream:* "Because they are so powerful." *Woman:* "Why am I afraid of power?—and so on. As the dialogue continues, and the insights become more profound, the problem very often solves itself.

Activity. Briefly describe what you wish to change at the beginning of the bridge, under "What You Are Now." Under "What You Want to Be," write in your goal. Work on one question at a time, as shown in the dream bridge, and write in the answer. Be patient; let the answers work on you before you proceed to the next question.